BRASS QUARTET
Score and Parts
-Trumpet
-Trumpet
-Trombone
-Tuba

I0559248

10 Christmas Songs FOR Brass Quartet

Jeff Bratz

Sign up for the HarmonyTabs email list to keep up with new music releases, upcoming publications, and promotions:

HARMONYTABS EMAIL LIST

10 CHRISTMAS SONGS FOR BRASS QUARTET
SECOND EDITION
Copyright © 2024 Jeff Bratz

To request permission, contact the publisher at publishing@HarmonyTabsMusic.com

ISBN: 978-1-961735-12-5 (paperback)
ISBN: 978-1-961735-13-2 (eBook)
ISMN: 979-0-60026-026-3 (paperback)
ISMN: 979-0-60026-027-0 (eBook)

First paperback edition October 2022

Printed in the United States of America

HarmonyTabs Music

HarmonyTabsMusic.com

CONTENTS

INTRO

First, thank you for buying this songbook. I know there are a lot of options out there and I'm honored you landed here.

I hope these songs will be as fun for you to play through as they were for me to arrange. I've always loved the holiday season and I think that's largely due to the music that fills the air in every store, car, home, and everywhere else. I like to believe that in some small part this book will add to the spirit.

On the last page of the score and on each part is a QR code. That code will lead you to a homepage for that song where you can find additional resources including audio/video where you can hear the tune and find optional rehearsal tracks.

If at any point you have any questions, comments, suggestions, or anything else, please feel free to drop me a line: Jeff@HarmonyTabs.com.

Happy music-ing!
-Jeff

ANGELS WE HAVE HEARD ON HIGH

Traditional French Carol
Arr. Jeff Bratz

AWHHOH (BQ)
11-11-24

ANGELS WE HAVE HEARD ON HIGH

AWHHOH (BQ)
11-11-24

AWHHOH (BQ)
11-11-24

ANGELS WE HAVE HEARD ON HIGH

1st Trumpet

Traditional French Carol
Arr. Jeff Bratz

ANGELS WE HAVE HEARD ON HIGH

2nd Trumpet

Traditional French Carol
Arr. Jeff Bratz

AWHHOH (BQ)
11-11-24

ANGELS WE HAVE HEARD ON HIGH

Trombone

Traditional French Carol
Arr. Jeff Bratz

ANGELS WE HAVE HEARD ON HIGH

Tuba

Traditional French Carol
Arr. Jeff Bratz

Additional resources for this arrangement

AWHHOH (BQ)
11-11-24

AULD LANG SYNE

Poem by Robert Burns
Arr. Jeff Bratz

AULD LANG SYNE

ALS (BQ)
11-11-24

1st Trumpet

AULD LANG SYNE

Poem by Robert Burns
Arr. Jeff Bratz

- 10 -

AULD LANG SYNE

POEM BY ROBERT BURNS
ARR. JEFF BRATZ

ALS (BQ)
11-11-24

AULD LANG SYNE

Trombone

Poem by Robert Burns
Arr. Jeff Bratz

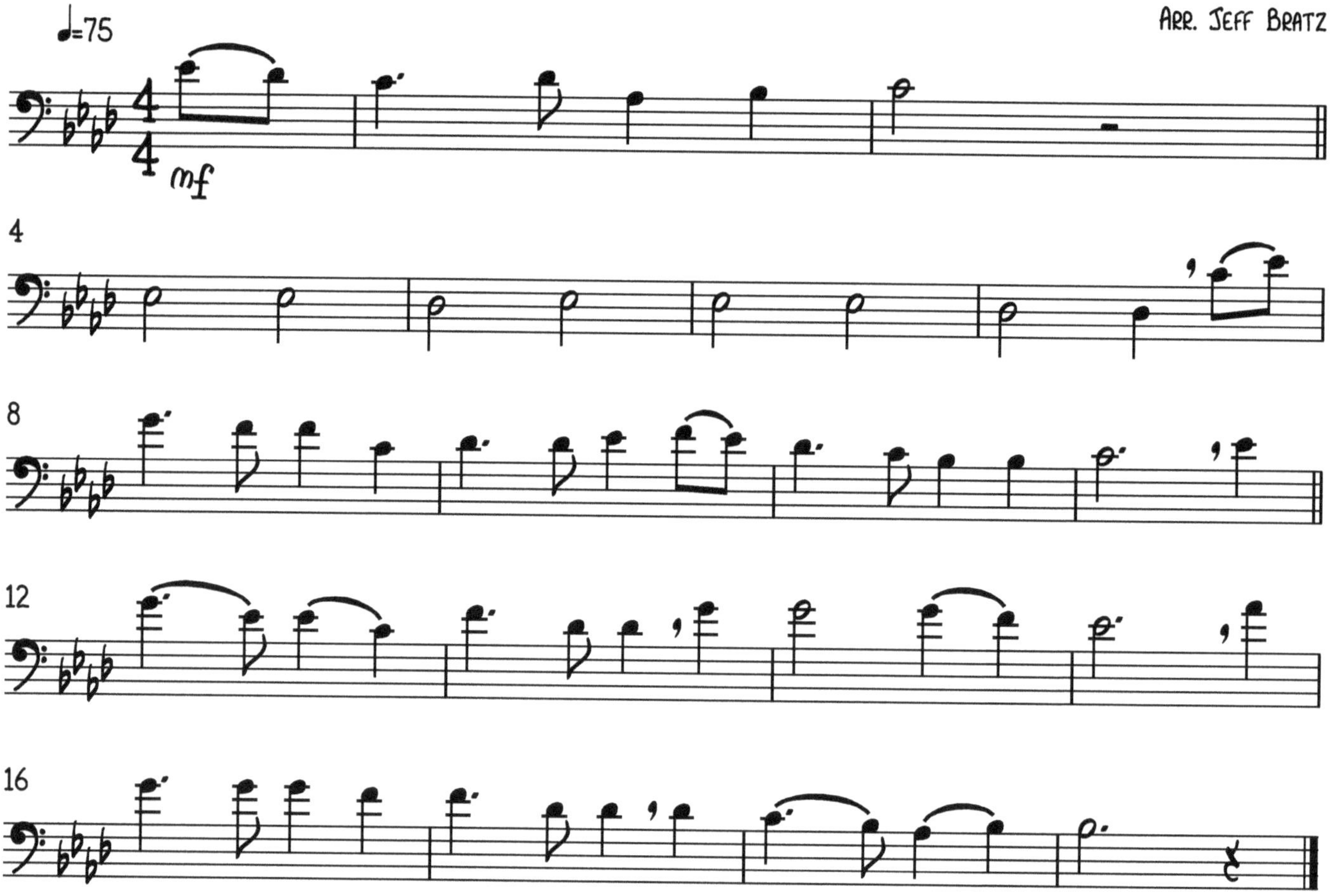

ALS (BQ)
11-11-24

- 12 -

Additional
resources for
this arrangement

TUBA

AULD LANG SYNE

POEM BY ROBERT BURNS
ARR. JEFF BRATZ

Additional resources for this arrangement

ALS (BQ)
11-11-24

AWAY IN A MANGER

William J. Kirkpatrick
and James R. Murray
Arr. Jeff Bratz

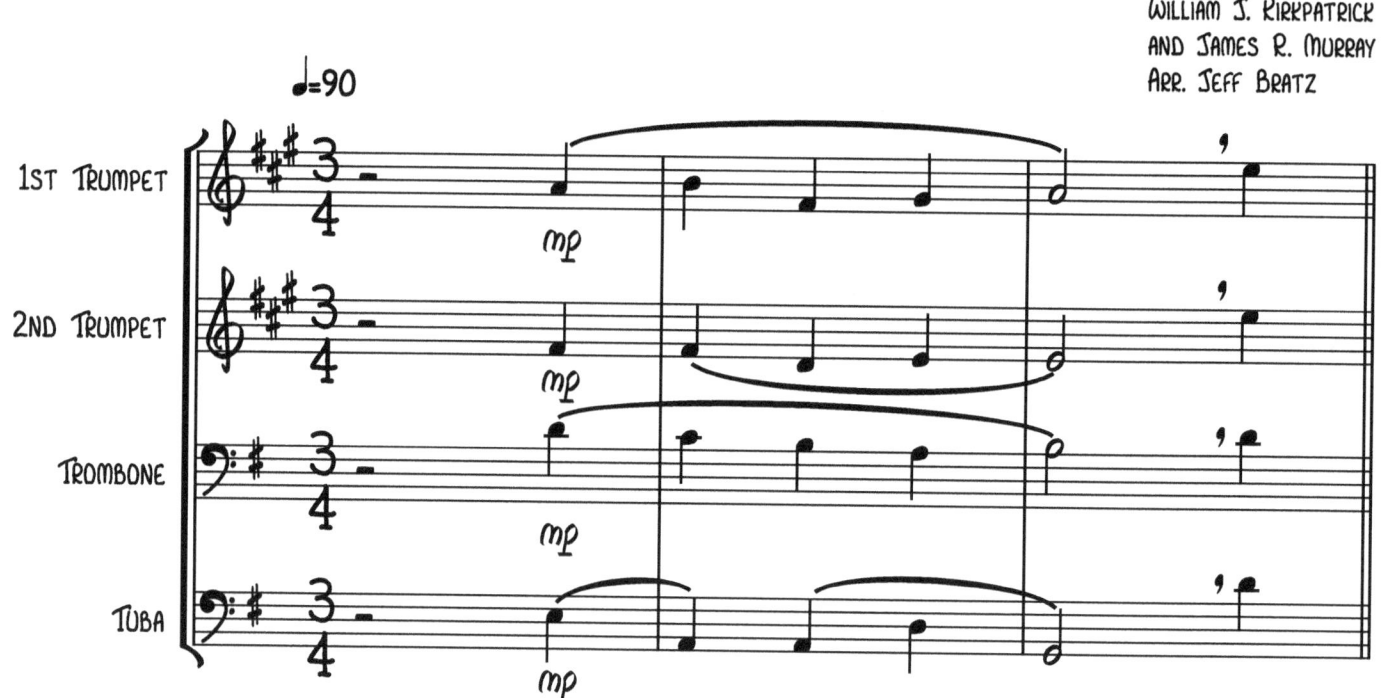

AIAM (BQ)
11-14-24

AWAY IN A MANGER

AIAM (BQ)
11-14-24

AWAY IN A MANGER

AWAY IN A MANGER

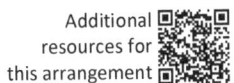
AIAM (BQ)
11-14-24

AIAM (BQ)
11-14-24

Additional resources for this arrangement

AWAY IN A MANGER

2ND TRUMPET

William J. Kirkpatrick
and James R. Murray
Arr. Jeff Bratz

Additional resources for this arrangement

AIAM (BQ)
11-14-24

AWAY IN A MANGER

Trombone

William J. Kirkpatrick
and James R. Murray
Arr. Jeff Bratz

AWAY IN A MANGER

Tuba

William J. Kirkpatrick
and James R. Murray
Arr. Jeff Bratz

AIAM (BQ)
11-14-24

DECK THE HALLS

Traditional Welsh Carol
Arr. Jeff Bratz

DTH (BQ)
11-15-24

- 22 -

DECK THE HALLS

DTH (BQ)
11-15-24

DECK THE HALLS

DECK THE HALLS

DTH (BQ)
11-15-24

DECK THE HALLS

DTH (BQ)
11-15-24

DECK THE HALLS

1st Trumpet

Traditional Welsh Carol
Arr. Jeff Bratz

DTH (BQ)
11-15-24

DECK THE HALLS

2nd Trumpet

Traditional Welsh Carol
Arr. Jeff Bratz

DTH (BQ)
11-15-24

DECK THE HALLS

Trombone

Traditional Welsh Carol
Arr. Jeff Bratz

DTH (BQ)
11-15-24

TROMBONE
DECK THE HALLS

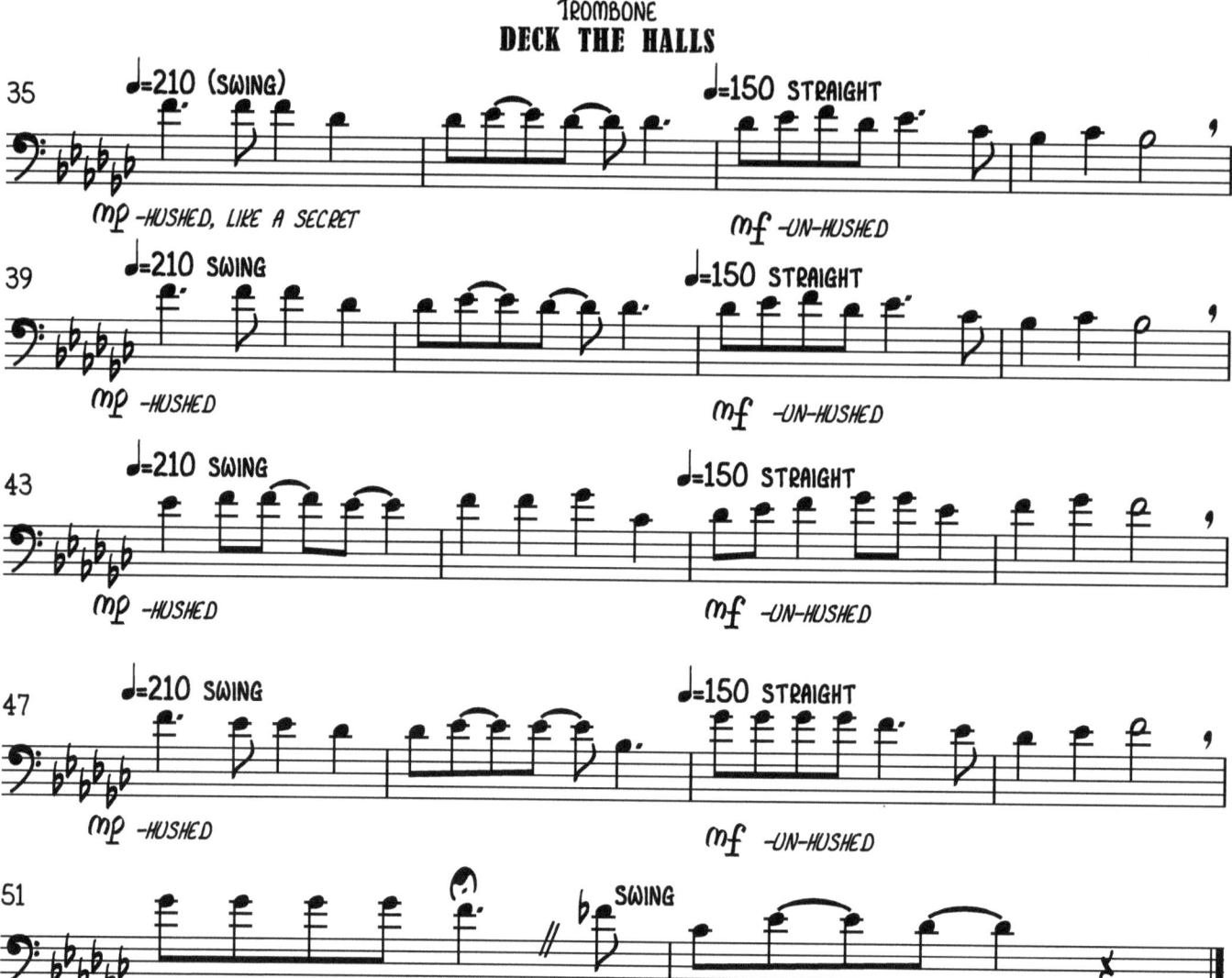

DTH (BQ)
11-15-24

DECK THE HALLS

DTH (BQ)
11-15-24

DECK THE HALLS

DTH (BQ)
11-15-24

THE FIRST NOEL

TRADITIONAL ENGLISH CAROL
ARR. JEFF BRATZ

TFN (BQ)
11-18-24

TFN (BQ)
11-18-24

THE FIRST NOEL

TFN (BQ)
11-18-24

THE FIRST NOEL

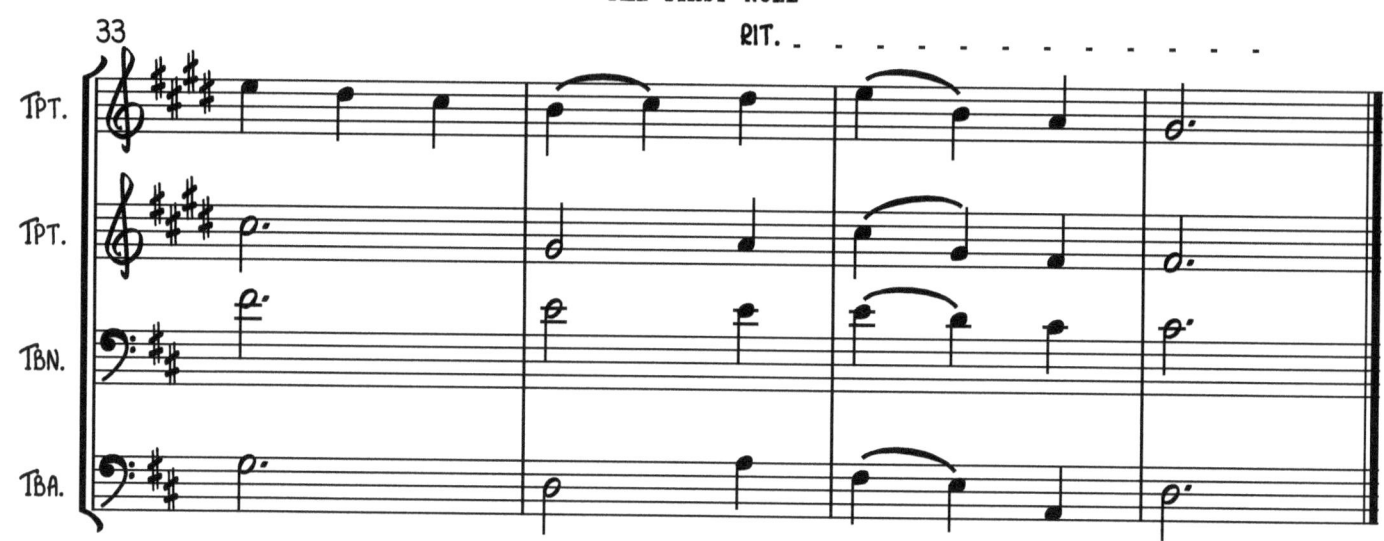

TFN (BQ)
11-18-24

THE FIRST NOEL

1st Trumpet

Traditional English Carol
Arr. Jeff Bratz

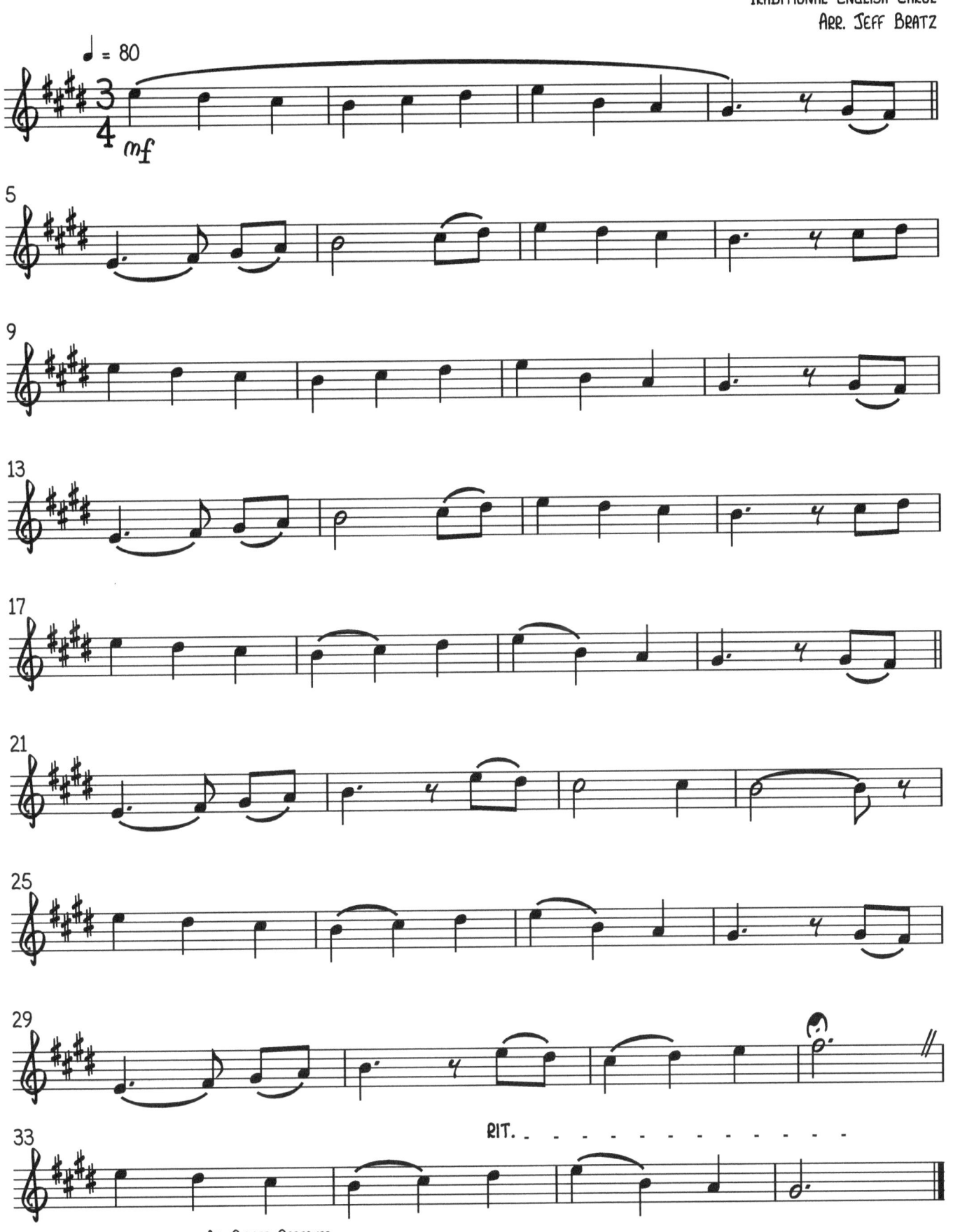

Additional resources for this arrangement

TFN (BQ)
11-18-24

THE FIRST NOEL

2nd Trumpet

Traditional English Carol
Arr. Jeff Bratz

TFN (BQ)
11-18-24

Additional
resources for
this arrangement

THE FIRST NOEL

Trombone

Traditional English Carol
Arr. Jeff Bratz

Additional resources for this arrangement

TFN (BQ)
11-18-24

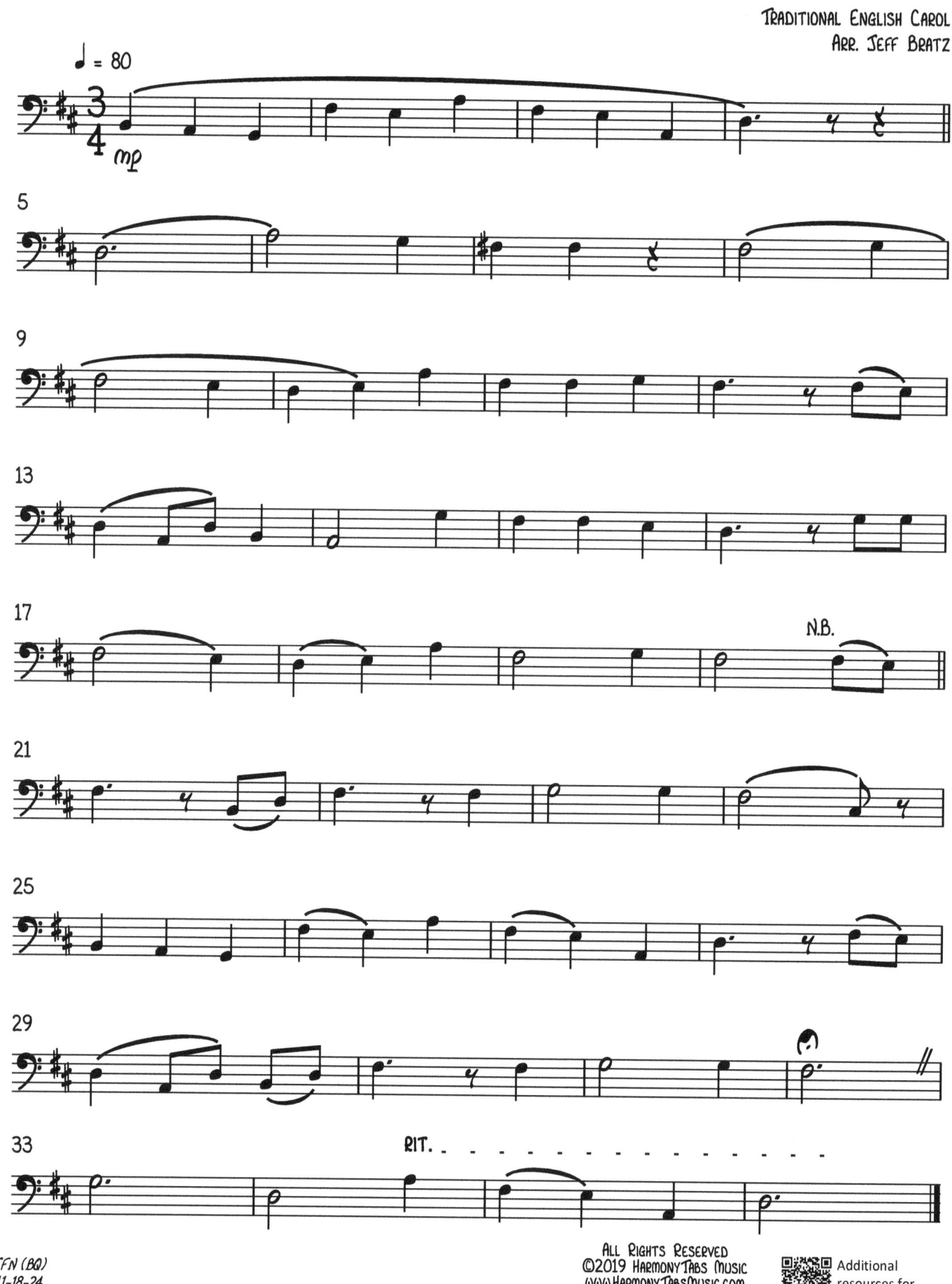

TFN (BQ)
11-18-24

Additional
resources for
this arrangement

GO TELL IT ON THE MOUNTAIN

COMPILED BY
JOHN WESLEY WORK, JR.
ARR. JEFF BRATZ

GT10TM (BQ)
11-21-24

GO TELL IT ON THE MOUNTAIN

GO TELL IT ON THE MOUNTAIN

GTIOTM (BQ)
11-21-24

GO TELL IT ON THE MOUNTAIN

GT 10TM (BQ)
11-21-24

GT10TM (BQ)
11-21-24

Additional resources for this arrangement

2ND TRUMPET
GO TELL IT ON THE MOUNTAIN

COMPILED BY
JOHN WESLEY WORK, JR.
ARR. JEFF BRATZ

♩=100 SWING

mf

TO CODA

D.S. AL CODA

CODA

N.B.

GT1OTM (BQ)
11-21-24

- 48 -

Additional
resources for
this arrangement

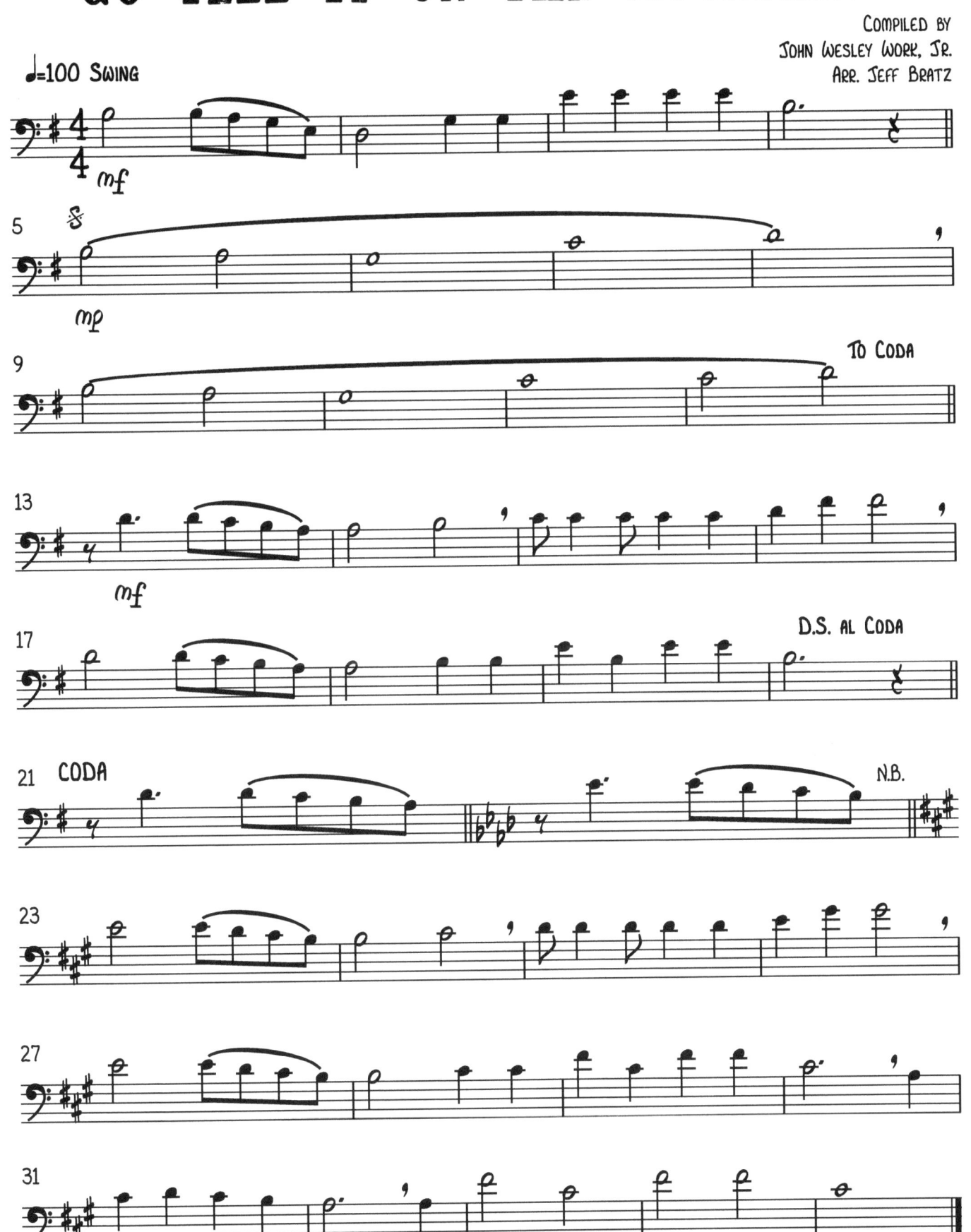

GO TELL IT ON THE MOUNTAIN

TROMBONE

COMPILED BY
JOHN WESLEY WORK, JR.
ARR. JEFF BRATZ

Additional resources for this arrangement

GT1OTM (BQ)
11-21-24

GO TELL IT ON THE MOUNTAIN

TUBA

COMPILED BY
JOHN WESLEY WORK, JR.
ARR. JEFF BRATZ

GOD REST YE MERRY, GENTLEMEN

19th Century English Carol
Arr. Jeff Bratz

GRYMG (BQ)
11-22-24

GOD REST YE MERRY, GENTLEMEN

GRY(mG (BQ)
11-22-24

GRY MG (BQ)
11-22-24

GOD REST YE MERRY, GENTLEMEN

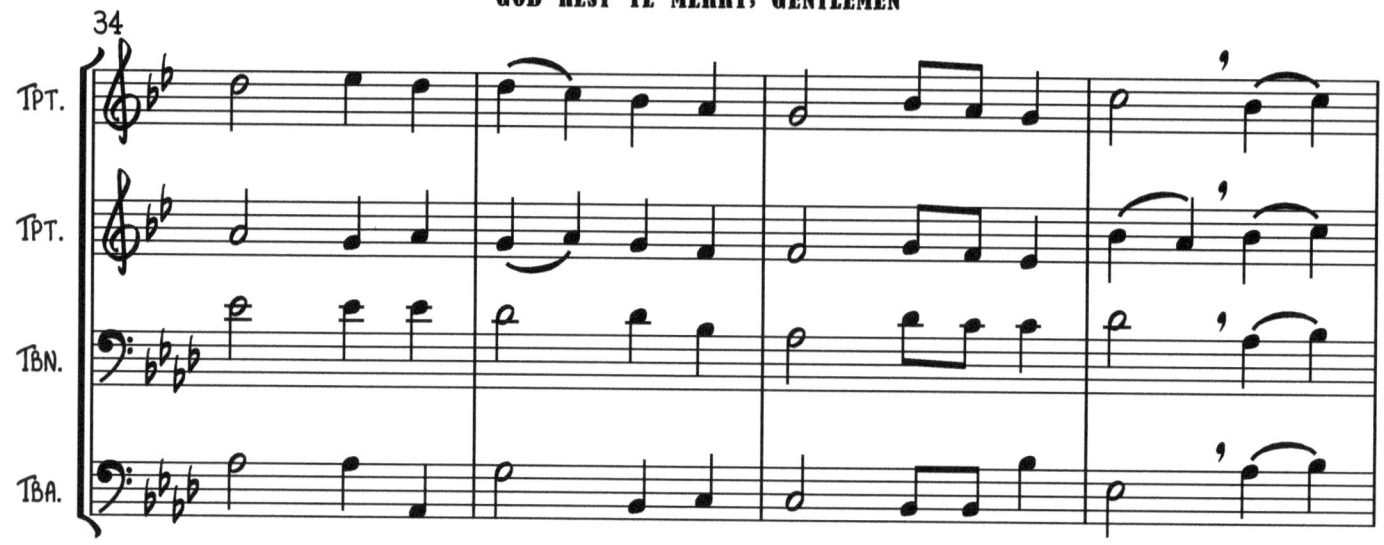

GOD REST YE MERRY, GENTLEMEN

1ST TRUMPET

19TH CENTURY ENGLISH CAROL
ARR. JEFF BRATZ

GRYMG (BQ)
11-22-24

GOD REST YE MERRY, GENTLEMEN

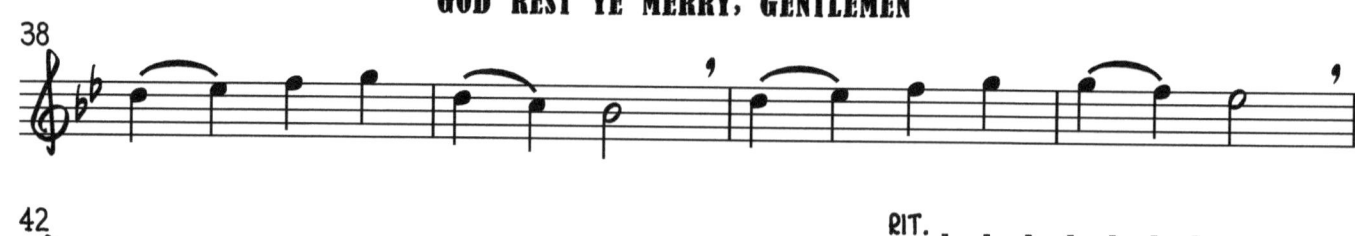

GRY(MG (BQ)
11-22-24

GOD REST YE MERRY, GENTLEMEN

2ND TRUMPET

19TH CENTURY ENGLISH CAROL
ARR. JEFF BRATZ

GRYmG (BQ)
11-22-24

GOD REST YE MERRY, GENTLEMEN

GOD REST YE MERRY, GENTLEMEN

Trombone

19th Century English Carol
Arr. Jeff Bratz

GRYMG (BQ)
11-22-24

GRYMG (BQ)
11-22-24

Additional resources for this arrangement

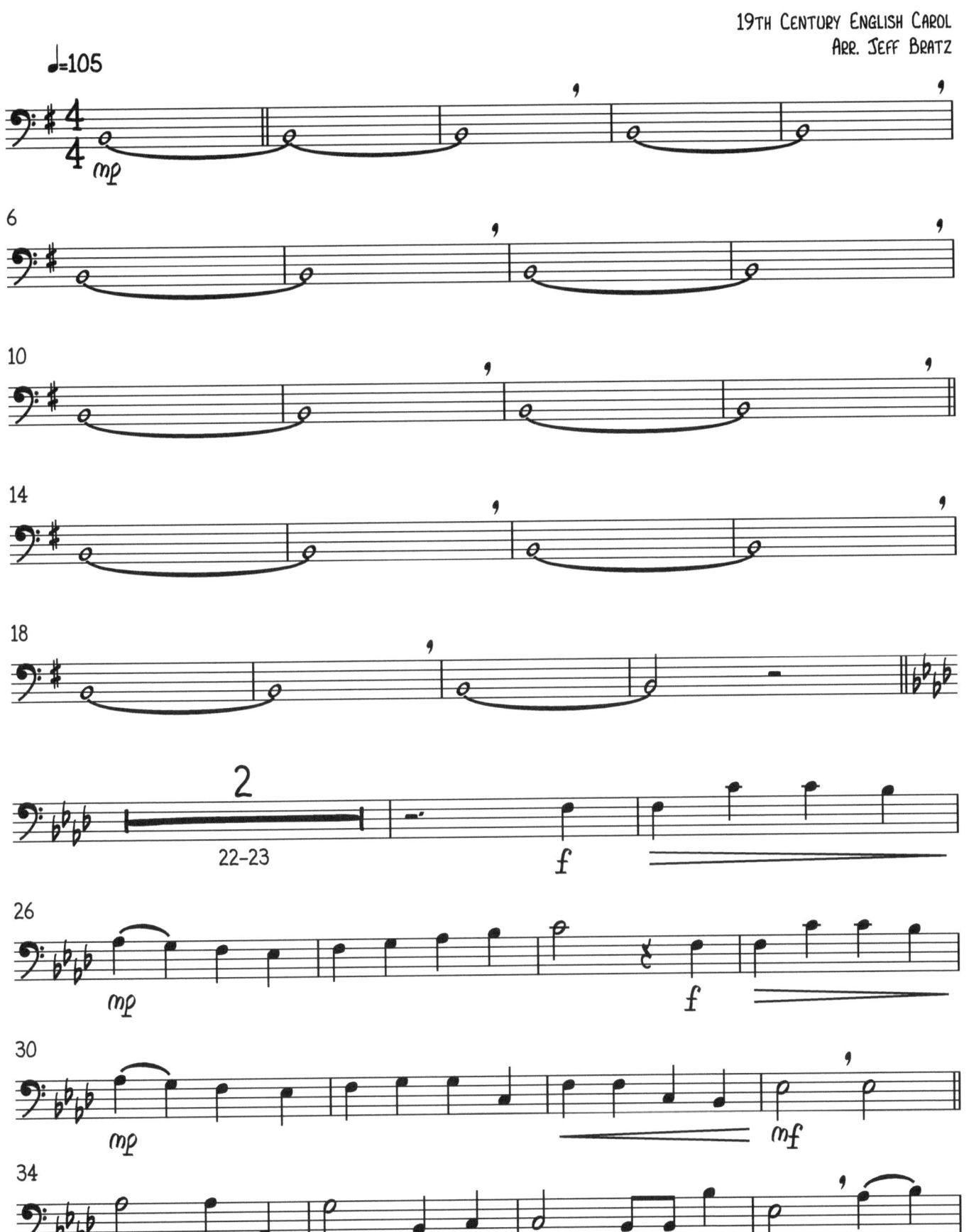

GOD REST YE MERRY, GENTLEMEN

TUBA

19TH CENTURY ENGLISH CAROL
ARR. JEFF BRATZ

GRYMG (BQ)
11-22-24

TUBA
GOD REST YE MERRY, GENTLEMEN

GRYMG (BQ)
11-22-24

HALLELUJAH CHORUS
(ABRIDGED)

George Friedrich Handel
Arr. Jeff Bratz

HC (BQ)
11-26-24

HALLELUJAH CHORUS (ABRIDGED)

HC (BQ)
11-26-24

HALLELUJAH CHORUS (ABRIDGED)

HC (BQ)
11-26-24

HALLELUJAH CHORUS (ABRIDGED)

HALLELUJAH CHORUS
(ABRIDGED)

1st Trumpet

George Friedrich Handel
Arr. Jeff Bratz

Additional resources for this arrangement

HC (BQ)
11-26-24

HALLELUJAH CHORUS
(ABRIDGED)

2ND TRUMPET

George Friedrich Handel
Arr. Jeff Bratz

HC (BQ)
11-26-24

Additional resources for this arrangement

Additional resources for this arrangement

HC (BQ)
11-26-24

HALLELUJAH CHORUS
(ABRIDGED)

Tuba

George Friedrich Handel
Arr. Jeff Bratz

HARK! THE HERALD ANGELS SING

Felix Mendelssohn
Lyrics by Charles Wesley
and George Whitefield
Arr. Jeff Bratz

HTHAS (BQ)
12-6-24

HTHAS (BQ)
12-6-24

HARK! THE HERALD ANGELS SING

HARK! THE HERALD ANGELS SING

1st Trumpet

Felix Mendelssohn
Lyrics by Charles Wesley
and George Whitefield
Arr. Jeff Bratz

HTHAS (BQ)
12-6-24

HARK! THE HERALD ANGELS SING

2ND TRUMPET

FELIX MENDELSSOHN
LYRICS BY CHARLES WESLEY
AND GEORGE WHITEFIELD
ARR. JEFF BRATZ

HTHAS (BQ)
12-6-24

Additional resources for this arrangement

HARK! THE HERALD ANGELS SING

Trombone

Felix Mendelssohn
Lyrics by Charles Wesley
and George Whitefield
Arr. Jeff Bratz

Additional resources for this arrangement

- 77 -

HTHAS (BQ)
12-6-24

HTHAS (BQ)
12-6-24

- 78 -

Additional
resources for
this arrangement

I SAW THREE SHIPS

Traditional
Arr. Jeff Bratz

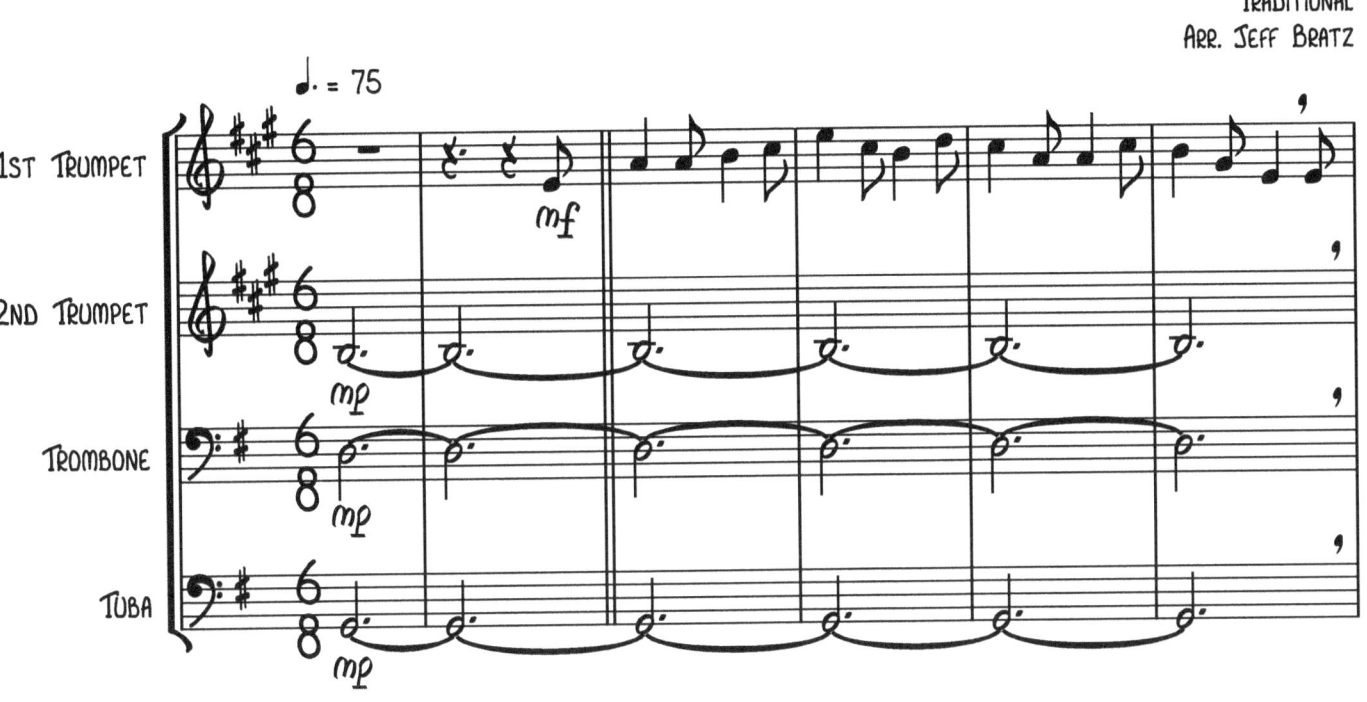

ISTS (BRQ)
12-16-24

I SAW THREE SHIPS

I SAW THREE SHIPS

ISTS (BrQ)
12-16-24

I SAW THREE SHIPS

I SAW THREE SHIPS

ISTS (BrQ)
12-16-24

I SAW THREE SHIPS

1st Trumpet

Traditional
Arr. Jeff Bratz

1STS (BRO)
12-16-24

I SAW THREE SHIPS

1ST'S (BQ)
12-16-24

I SAW THREE SHIPS

TRADITIONAL
ARR. JEFF BRATZ

ISTS (BRQ)
12-16-24

ISMN: 979-0-60026-036-2

I SAW THREE SHIPS

 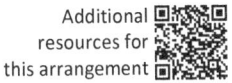

ISTS (BrQ)
12-16-24

I SAW THREE SHIPS

Trombone

Traditional
Arr. Jeff Bratz

I SAW THREE SHIPS

ISTS (BbQ)
12-16-24

Tuba

Traditional
Arr. Jeff Bratz

I SAW THREE SHIPS

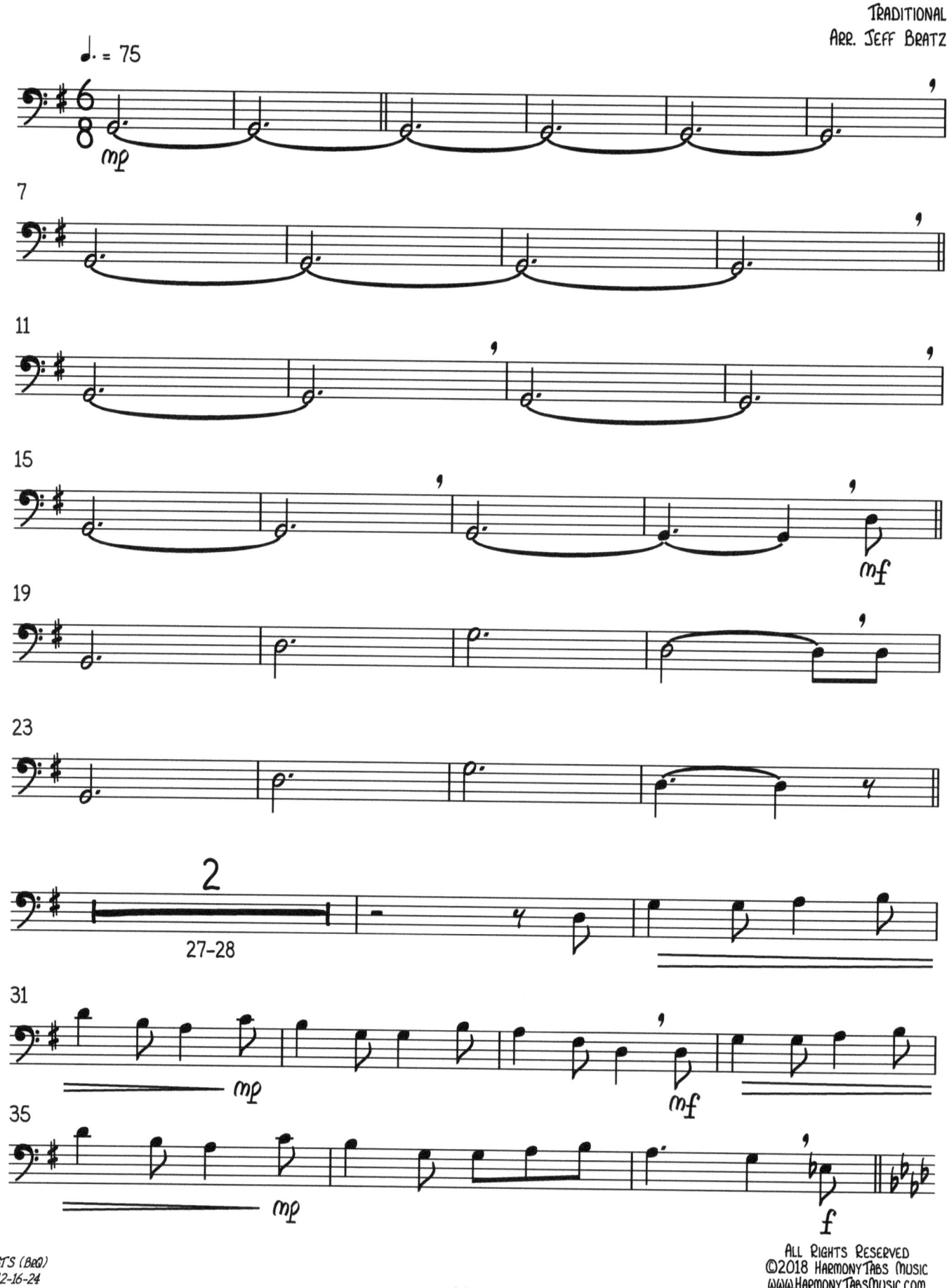

ISTS (Bro)
12-16-24

ISTS (BrQ)
12-16-24

FINAL WORDS

Please consider leaving a review of this book. I would greatly appreciate it. It will help me to continue on this book writing journey I've set off on.

Thank you in advance!

Leave a Review

HARMONYTABS EMAIL LIST

Once again, here is the link to the HarmonyTabs email list to keep you up to speed on any new music, publications, and promotions.

ABOUT THE AUTHOR

Jeff Bratz has a degree in Professional Music from the School for Music Vocations and a Professional Certificate in Music Theory and Composition from Berklee College of Music. He's a composer and arranger specializing in vocal arrangements. In a former life, Jeff was a music teacher for grades pre-k through high school. He has sung in dozens of vocal groups including The Dickens Carolers at Disneyland's *Club 33*, The Fault Line on *America's Got Talent*, and Manhattan Transfer tribute group LA Transfer. He was also part of the Downbeat award-winning First Take. He currently performs with rock band RaDIUM, 80s rock tribute band 8IGHTY 6IXX, and salsa band Calle Mambo. He lives in Massachusetts with his wonderful partner Kristen and the cutest nugget that ever nuggeted: Ollie!

Also Available From

HarmonyTabs

Sheet Music

-A Cappella Choirs/Groups
-Brass Ensembles
-String Ensembles
-Sax Ensembles
And More!

HARMONYTABS.COM/SHEET-MUSIC/

Songbooks

-Wind Ensembles
-A Cappella Choirs/Groups
-Flute Ensembles
-Brass Ensembles
And More!

HARMONYTABS.COM/MUSIC-BOOKS/SONGBOOKS/

Music Theory and Instruction

-An Incomplete Crash Course
In Contemporary Music Theory:
The Fundamentals

More to Come!

HARMONYTABS.COM/MUSIC-BOOKS/INSTRUCTIONAL-BOOKS/

Music Composition

-Standard Manuscript Notebook
-Pocket Manuscript Notebook
-Writing Prompt Journals

More to Come!

HARMONYTABS.COM/MUSIC-BOOKS/MUSIC-COMPOSITION-BOOKS/

HarmonyTabsMusic.com